PRE-ACCREDITATION
MATHS & LITERACY FOR
BUSINESS ADMIN

Graduated exercises and practice exam

Andrew Spencer

A+ National Pre-accreditation Maths & Literacy for Business Admin
1st Edition
Andrew Spencer

Publishing editors: Jane Moylan and Jana Raus
Editor: Kerry Nagle
Senior designer: Vonda Pestana
Cover design: Vonda Pestana
Text design: Vonda Pestana
Cover image: iStockphoto
Photo research: UC Publishing
Production controller: Jo Vraca and Damian Almeida
Reprint: Katie McCappin
Typeset by UC Publishing Pty Ltd

Any URLs contained in this publication were checked for currency during the production process. Note, however, that the publisher cannot vouch for the ongoing currency of URLs.

Acknowledgements
We would like to thank the following for permission to reproduce copyright material:

iStockphotos: p2 Imagesby Trista, p8 laflor, p10 Gewoldi, p11 eyecrave, p12 best-photo, p13 MJHollinshead, p14 himbeertoni, p15 sjlocke, p16 craftvision, p17 NejroN, p20 nyul, p21 JerryPDX, p23 narvikk, p27 Lighthousebay, p30 Snowleopard1, p31 sampsyseeds.

For product information and technology assistance,
in Australia call **1300 790 853**;
in New Zealand call **0800 449 725**

For permission to use material from this text or product, please email **aust.permissions@cengage.com**

ISBN 978 0 17 047386 6

Cengage Learning Australia
Level 7, 80 Dorcas Street
South Melbourne, Victoria Australia 3205

Cengage Learning New Zealand
Unit 4B Rosedale Office Park
331 Rosedale Road, Albany, North Shore 0632, NZ

For learning solutions, visit **cengage.com.au**

Printed in Australia by Ligare Pty Limited.
1 2 3 4 5 6 7 26 25 24 23 22

A+ National

PRE-ACCREDITATION

Maths & Literacy for Business Admin

Contents

Introduction   v
About the author   vi
Acknowledgements   vi

LITERACY		
Unit 1	Spelling	1
Unit 2	Alphabetising	2
Unit 3	Comprehension	3

MATHEMATICS		
Unit 4	General Mathematics	5
Unit 5	Basic Operations	9
	Section A: Addition	
	Section B: Subtraction	
	Section C: Multiplication	
	Section D: Division	
Unit 6	Decimals	14
	Section A: Addition	
	Section B: Subtraction	
	Section C: Multiplication	
	Section D: Division	
Unit 7	Fractions	19
	Section A: Addition	
	Section B: Subtraction	
	Section C: Multiplication	
	Section D: Division	
Unit 8	Percentages	22
Unit 9	Measurement Conversions	24

Unit 10	Earning Wages	26
Unit 11	Squaring Numbers	28
	Section A: Introducing square numbers	
	Section B: Applying square numbers to the trade	
Unit 12	Invoices/Bills/Specials	31
Unit 13	Practice Written Exam for the Business Admin Trade	33

Glossary 42
Formulae and Data 43
Notes 46

Introduction

It has always been important to understand, from a teacher's perspective, the nature of the mathematical skills students need for their future, rather than teaching them textbook mathematics. This has been a guiding principle behind the development of the content in this workbook. To teach maths that is *relevant* to students seeking employement is the best that we can do, to give students an education in the field that they would like to work in.

The content in this resource is aimed at the level that is needed for a student to have the best possibility of improving their maths and literacy skills specifically for Business Administration. Students can use this workbook to prepare for an entry assessment, or even to assist with basic numeracy and literacy at the VET/TAFE level. Coupled with the NelsonNet website, https://www.nelsonnet.com.au/free-resources, these resources have the potential to improve the students' understanding of basic mathematical concepts that can be applied to trades. These resources have been trialled, and they work.

Commonly used work terms are introduced so that students have a basic understanding of terminology they will encounter in the workplace environment. Students who can complete this workbook and reach an 80 per cent or higher outcome in all topics will have achieved the goal of this resource. These students will go on to complete work experience, do a VET accredited course, or be able to gain entry into VET/TAFE or an apprenticeship in the trade of their choice.

The content in this workbook is the first step towards bridging the gap between what has been learnt in previous years, and what needs to be remembered and re-learnt for use at work. Students will significantly benefit from the consolidation of the basic maths and literacy concepts.

Every school has students who want to work with their hands, and not all students want to go to university. The best students want to learn what they don't know, and if students want to learn, then this book has the potential to give them a good start in life.

This resource has been specifically tailored to prepare students for sitting VET/TAFE admission tests, and for giving students the basic skills they will need for a career in trade. In many ways, it is a win-win situation, with students enjoying and studying relevant maths for work and VET/TAFE receiving students that have improved basic maths and literacy skills.

All that is needed is patience, hard work, a positive attitude, a belief in yourself that you can do it and a desire to achieve. The rest is up to you.

About the author

Andrew Spencer has studied education both within Australia and overseas. He has a Bachelor of Education, as well as a Masters of Science in which he specialised in teacher education. Andrew has extensive experience in teaching secondary mathematics throughout New South Wales and South Australia for well over fifteen years. He has taught a range of subject areas including Maths, English, Science, Classics, Physical Education and Technical Studies. His sense of the importance of practical mathematics continued to develop with the range of subject areas he taught in.

Acknowledgements

For Paula, Zach, Katelyn, Mum and Dad.
Many thanks to Mal Aubrey (GTA) and all training organisations for their input.
    To the De La Salle Brothers for their selfless work with all students.
    Thanks also to Dr. Pauline Carter for her unwavering support for all maths teachers.
    This is for all students who value learning, who are willing to work hard and who have character … and are characters!

LITERACY

Unit 1: Spelling

Short-answer questions

Specific instructions to students

- This is an exercise to help you to identify and correct spelling errors.
- Read the activity below, then answer accordingly.

Read the following passage and identify and correct the spelling errors:

A receptionst arives at the office at 8.45 a.m. There are three apointments for clients between 9.00 a.m. and 9.30 a.m. They begin proparing for a busy Friday, as this is usually the day of the week that the payroll and banking are done. Once the appointment book is cheked, the receptionist begins to look over the acounts payeble and acounts recievable. Several accounts need to be paid so the receptionist begins on them imediately. The payroll needed to be double-checked, to make sure all payment records were acurate. This ensured that all employes would get paid on time and everyone would receve their pay. Once this was completed, the receptionist started on the banking. The petty cash box was checked for invoyces and any other cover notes that show that money had been taken from the box. All the money balanced out and the banking of the petty cash could be done later that day.

The recetionist began preparing morning tea for the managor and the clients that he had been in a conferance with during the early part of the day. Special care was taken with the food preperation as in the previous week several staff had come down with food poisoning and the managemant had sent out a memo asking all staff to be diligant about washing their hands before preparing food.

Incorrect words:

_____

_____

Correct words:

_____

_____

Unit 2: Alphabetising

Short-answer questions

Specific instructions to students

- In this unit, you will be able to practise your alphabetising skills.
- Read the activity below, then answer accordingly.

Put the following words into alphabetical order:

management	adjustment note	accounts payable	appointments
financial reports	tax invoice	invoices	customer service
general ledger	receiving goods	delivery docket	revenue
payroll processing	petty cash		

Answer:

_____

_____

_____

_____

_____

_____

_____

_____

_____

_____

_____

Short-answer questions

Specific instructions to students

- This is an exercise to help you understand what you read.
- Read the following activity, then answer the questions that follow.

Read the following passage and answer the questions in sentence form.

It was 11.45 a.m., nearing lunchtime and Suzette, who was the receptionist, was looking forward to having a break. Ivy, the Accounts Manager, entered the front office with a wad of papers in her hand. She spoke to Suzette and said that a number of urgent tasks had come up. Ivy gave the papers to Suzette and she pointed out that there were several indiscretions in the balance of the petty cash book. The credits and debits did not balance. Ivy had placed a number of receipts away in her drawer but had not forwarded them on to administration. Suzette immediately began dividing up the papers into three separate piles: receipts for petty cash, invoices and delivery dockets. Somehow the different papers had been mixed together and there was no order to them.

By two o'clock, Suzette had everything under control. Fortunately, she had great administrative skills and she had also developed a wonderful ability to problem solve. Ivy returned at 3.00 p.m. and Suzette explained that she had balanced the petty cash book and recorded all invoices on the database on the computer. Suzette had also filed copies of all paperwork and organised the delivery dockets into the dates and times that parcels and orders had arrived and were sent. Both Ivy and Suzette were pleased that they were able to catch up with the work but vowed to have a better system in place in the future. Suzette suggested that all paperwork be placed in an 'in' tray as it arrived so that she could keep up with all paperwork on a daily basis. Ivy agreed with her suggestion.

QUESTION 1

What was the problem with the petty cash book?

Answer:

QUESTION 2

What was the problem with the receipts and paperwork?

Answer:

QUESTION 3

How long did it take for Suzette to get everything 'under control'?

Answer:

_____

QUESTION 4

How did Suzette overcome the problems with the urgent tasks?

Answer:

_____

_____

QUESTION 5

What was Suzette's suggestion for the future so that the same problem was not repeated?

Answer:

_____

9780170473866

MATHEMATICS

Unit 4: General Mathematics

Short-answer questions

Specific instructions to students

- This unit will help you to improve your general mathematical skills.
- Read the following questions and answer all of them in the spaces provided.
- You may not use a calculator.
- You need to show all working.

QUESTION 1

What unit of measurement would you use to measure:

a   the length of a desktop?

Answer:

_____

b   the temperature of air conditioning?

Answer:

_____

c   the amount of money in petty cash?

Answer:

_____

d   the weight of a receptionist's chair?

Answer:

_____

e   the voltage of an appliance (such as a coffee maker)?

Answer:

_____

QUESTION 2

Write an example of the following and where it may be found in the business administration industry:

a   percentages

Answer:

_____

b   decimals

Answer:

_____

c   fractions

Answer:

_____

d   mixed numbers

Answer:

_____

e   ratios

Answer:

_____

_____

f   angles

Answer:

_____

_____

QUESTION 3

Convert the following units:

a 12 kg to grams

Answer:

b 4 t to kilograms

Answer:

c 120 cm to metres

Answer:

d 1140 mL to litres

Answer:

e 1650 g to kilograms

Answer:

f 1880 kg to tonnes

Answer:

g 13 m to centimetres

Answer:

h 4.5 L to millitres

Answer:

QUESTION 4

Write the following in descending order:

0.4   0.04   4.1   40.0   400.00   4.0

Answer:

QUESTION 5

Write the decimal number that is between the following:

a 0.2 and 0.4

Answer:

b 1.8 and 1.9

Answer:

c 12.4 and 12.5

Answer:

d 28.3 and 28.4

Answer:

e 101.5 and 101.7

Answer:

QUESTION 6

Round off the following numbers to two decimal places:

a 12.346

Answer:

b 2.251

Answer:

c 123.897

Answer:

d 688.882

Answer:

e 1209.741

Answer:

QUESTION 7

Estimate the following by approximation:

a $1288 \times 19 =$

Answer:

___

b $201 \times 20 =$

Answer:

___

c $497 \times 12.2 =$

Answer:

___

d $1008 \times 10.3 =$

Answer:

___

e $399 \times 22 =$

Answer:

___

f $201 - 19 =$

Answer:

___

g $502 - 61 =$

Answer:

___

h $1003 - 49 =$

Answer:

___

i $10\ 001 - 199 =$

Answer:

___

j $99.99 - 39.8 =$

Answer:

___

QUESTION 8

What do the following add up to?

a $4, $4.99 and $144.95

Answer:

___

b   8.75, 6.9 and 12.55

Answer:

___

c   65 mL, 18 mL and 209 mL

Answer:

___

d   21.3 g, 119 g and 884.65 g

Answer:

___

QUESTION 9

Subtract the following:

a   2338 from 7117

Answer:

___

b   1786 from 3112

Answer:

___

c   5979 from 8014

Answer:

___

d   11 989 from 26 221

Answer:

___

e   108 767 from 231 111

Answer:

___

Use division to solve the following:

a   2177 ÷ 7 =

Answer:

_____

b   4484 ÷ 4 =

Answer:

_____

c   63.9 ÷ 0.3 =

Answer:

_____

d   121.63 ÷ 1.2 =

Answer:

_____

e   466.88 ÷ 0.8 =

Answer:

_____

The following information is provided for Question 11.

To solve using BODMAS, in order from left to right, solve the Brackets first, then Of, then Division, then Multiplication, then Addition and lastly Subtraction. The following example has been done for your reference.

EXAMPLE:

Solve (4 × 7) × 2 + 6 − 4.

_____

STEP 1

Solve the Brackets first: (4 × 7) = 28

STEP 2

No Division so next solve Multiplication: 28 × 2 = 56

STEP 3

Addition is next: 56 + 6 = 62

STEP 4

Subtraction is the last process: 62 − 4 = 58

_____

FINAL ANSWER

58

Using BODMAS, solve:

a   (6 × 9) × 5 + 7 − 2 =

Answer:

_____

b   (9 × 8) × 4 + 6 − 1 =

Answer:

_____

c   3 × (5 × 7) + 11 − 8 =

Answer:

_____

d   5 × (8 × 3) + 9 − 6 =

Answer:

_____

e   7 + 6 × 3 + (9 × 6) − 9 =

Answer:

_____

f   6 + 9 × 4 + (6 × 7) − 21 =

Answer:

_____

Section A: Addition

Short-answer questions

Specific instructions to students

- This section will help you to improve your addition skills for basic operations.
- Read the questions below and answer all of them in the spaces provided.
- You may not use a calculator.
- You need to show all working.

QUESTION 1

A receptionist tends to three petty cash vouchers. The vouchers are for 2 L of milk costing $3, a jar of coffee costing $8 and a packet of biscuits for $5. What would the total be?

Answer:

_____

QUESTION 2

Four petty cash vouchers contain the following details: stationery costing $60, postage stamps totalling $18, envelopes costing $12 and sandwiches for a luncheon costing $50. What is the total?

Answer:

_____

QUESTION 3

A front office does a stocktake and finds the following items in stock: 127 pens, 26 manila folders and 32 binders. How many items are in stock, in total?

Answer:

_____

QUESTION 4

An administration assistant purchases the following for the office: cleaning products for $35, coffee, tea and sugar for $45, envelopes for $17 and a box of staples, paper clips and a hole punch for $19. How much in total has been spent?

Answer:

_____

QUESTION 5

An administrative assistant takes the following amount of time to file documents: employee personal details – 13 minutes, medical files – 14 minutes, patient files – 17 minutes and Medicare documents – 23 minutes.

a How much time has been taken, in minutes?

Answer:

_____

b How much time has been taken in hours and minutes?

Answer:

_____

QUESTION 6

A receptionist purchases the following items: three binders for $25, two jars of coffee for $35, 10 bottles of purified water for $45 and 20 display folders for $25. How much money has been spent?

Answer:

_____

QUESTION 7

An employee submits the following vouchers to the receptionist for reimbursement after a day conference that was interstate: two vouchers for taxi fares totalling $115, food costing $25, drinks with staff from other companies for $89 and the fee to attend the conference paid on the day costing $65. How much is the total reimbursement?

Answer:

_____

QUESTION 8

On Friday, the receptionist balances cash in the petty cash box. The box has 2 × $50 notes, 4 × $20 notes, 3 × $10 notes, 9 × $5 notes, 12 × $2 coins and 11 × $1 coins. What is the total?

Answer:

QUESTION 9

An administrative assistant is asked to balance the following amounts of cash and coin that has been received by a small company: 6 × $50 notes, 9 × $20 notes, 15 × $10 notes, 19 × $5 notes, 26 × $2 coins and 38 × $1 coins. What is the total?

Answer:

QUESTION 10

A company has a fundraiser for a charity. The following amounts are received and need to be counted: 5 × $50 notes, 22 × $20 notes, 133 × $10 notes, 14 × $5 notes, 129 × $2 coins and 163 × $1 coins. How much did the company raise for the charity?

Answer:

Section B: Subtraction

Short-answer questions

Specific instructions to students

- This section will help you to improve your subtraction skills for basic operations.
- Read the following questions and answer all of them in the spaces provided.
- You may not use a calculator.
- You need to show all working.

QUESTION 1

An office purchases a range of stationary that costs $12. How much change is given from $50?

Answer:

QUESTION 2

Four document wallets and a box of overhead transparency sheets are bought for an office at a cost of $43. How much change will be given from $100?

Answer:

QUESTION 3

A receptionist purchases the following office supplies: five packets of AAA batteries for $9, 24 whiteboard markers for $41 and six glue sticks for $15. How much change will be given from $100?

Answer:

QUESTION 4

An office uses 27 whiteboard markers from a box that contains 100 whiteboard markers. How many are left in the box?

Answer:

QUESTION 5

The total cost of office supplies for the period of January to June comes to $425. The bill is paid from petty cash using 10 × $50 notes. How much change should be received?

Answer:

QUESTION 6

A company uses 31 display folders from a box that contains 50 display folders. How many are left in the box?

Answer:

QUESTION 7

A luncheon for management costs $135. The receptionist pays for it from petty cash using three $50 notes. How much change will she receive?

Answer:

QUESTION 8

An administrative assistant purchases stock for a paper company. The total cost comes to $68. Two $50 notes are used from petty cash to pay for the purchases. How much change is received?

Answer:

QUESTION 9

A receptionist purchases the following items for the office: 12 AA batteries for $9, six packets of staples for $7 and 10 whiteboard markers for $17. If there was $211 in the petty cash box before paying for the purchases, how much money remains after payment is completed?

Answer:

QUESTION 10

An office purchases 24 display folders for $34, two pads of grid paper for $5, five glue sticks for $11 and 50 whiteboard markers of various colours for $85. If there was $302 in petty cash prior to the purchases, how much will be left after the purchases?

Answer:

Section C: Multiplication

Short-answer questions

Specific instructions to students

- This section will help you to improve your multiplication skills for basic operations.
- Read the following questions and answer all of them in the spaces provided.
- You may not use a calculator.
- You need to show all working.

QUESTION 1

If document wallets cost $3 each, how much would 25 document wallets cost?

Answer:

QUESTION 2

If black pens cost $2 each, how much would 75 black pens cost?

Answer:

QUESTION 3

Management puts on four luncheons in a month. Each luncheon costs $37. What will the total cost be for a month?

Answer:

QUESTION 4

Each month the cost for coffee, tea, milk and sugar comes to $28. What is the total cost for six months worth of these items?

Answer:

QUESTION 5

Each month a set of documents need to be posted to an interstate company. Each time they are posted it costs $9. What would be the total expenditure for posting the items over a 15-month period?

Answer:

_____

QUESTION 6

A group of seven visitors take two taxis to the city from the airport for a meeting. The cost for each taxi comes to $39. What is the total for both taxis?

Answer:

_____

QUESTION 7

A cheque for $237 is made out each month to a cleaning company for cleaning the offices. How much is spent on cleaning for a year?

Answer:

_____

QUESTION 8

A water filtration system for a large company requires servicing quarterly. Each service costs $65. How much does the administrative assistant make the cheque out for at the end of each financial year?

Answer:

_____

QUESTION 9

Twelve new leather chairs are purchased for a company's boardroom. Each chair costs $185. How much will the total be?

Answer:

QUESTION 10

A receptionist purchases five coffee tables. If each one costs $87, how much will all five cost?

Answer:

_____

Section D: Division

Short-answer questions

Specific instructions to students

- This section will help you to improve your division skills for basic operations.
- Read the following questions and answer all of them in the spaces provided.
- You may not use a calculator.
- You need to show all working.

QUESTION 1

If five items of furniture are purchased for $110, how much will the unit cost be for each?

Answer:

_____

QUESTION 2

If a receptionist earns $568 (before tax) for working a five-day week, how much would the receptionist earn per day?

Answer:

_____

QUESTION 3

A purchasing officer purchases four chairs for an office and the total comes to $260. How much does each chair cost?

Answer:

QUESTION 4

A receptionist purchases eight AA batteries for $6. What is the unit cost?

Answer:

QUESTION 5

A company sends 12 documents using priority post to an interstate company at a cost of $156. How much does each document cost to send?

Answer:

QUESTION 6

A company's income totals $15 699 for three weeks. What is the average weekly income for this period?

Answer:

QUESTION 7

A company spends $371 on seven luncheons for meetings. How much does each luncheon cost?

Answer:

QUESTION 8

There are 36 people invited to the opening of a new trade facility. Nibbles and drinks are provided for the visitors and the bill comes to $828. What is the cost per person?

Answer:

QUESTION 9

A company has 12 employees. The total of their wages comes to $390 000. What is the average wage per person?

Answer:

QUESTION 10

A company employs 20 workers. The total of their wages comes to $540 000. What is the average wage per worker?

Answer:

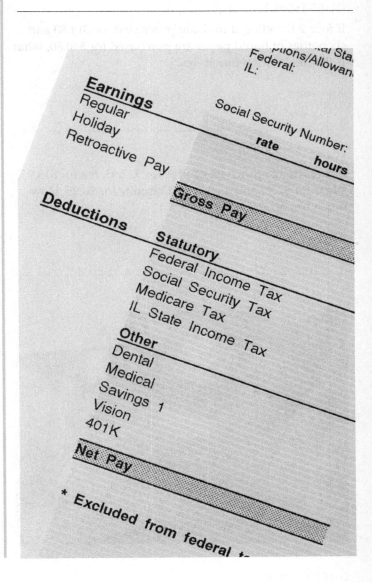

Unit 6: Decimals

Section A: Addition

Short-answer questions

Specific instructions to students

- This section will help you to improve your addition skills when working with decimals.
- Read the following questions and answer all of them in the spaces provided.
- You may not use a calculator.
- You need to show all working.

QUESTION 1

If four 2 L bottles of milk are purchased for $14.80 and six bottles of liquid paper are purchased for $40.80, what is the total for the purchases?

Answer:

QUESTION 2

A receptionist purchases coffee for $22.95, tea for $18.95, sugar for $2.95 and a packet of biscuits for $6.95. How much has been spent?

Answer:

QUESTION 3

A new water cooler costs $62.50 and cups cost $13.95. How much does the order come to?

Answer:

QUESTION 4

A 12-pack of binders is purchased for $71.40 as well as six packets of staples for $10.50. How much is the total?

Answer:

QUESTION 5

A company forwards documents by courier to three clients. The cost of the service to each client by the courier is $14.75, $8.95 and $21.50 respectively. How much is the total cost for forwarding the documents?

Answer:

QUESTION 6

A company receives cheques from four clients. The amount of each cheque is $220.50, $150.85, $135.50 and $189.90. How much do the cheques total?

Answer:

QUESTION 7

A receptionist purchases furniture for an office. The main table costs $345.50, four chairs cost $165.95 as a set and a coffee table is purchased for $59.95. What total should the cheque be made out for?

Answer:

QUESTION 8

Five patients at a dentist have different procedures. The cost of each procedure is $86.50, $135.50, $110.25, $347.90 and $1198.50. What will the total for all of the procedures come to?

Answer:

QUESTION 9

A medical receptionist receives four different items for use in the practice. All goods arrive separately. The items cost $78.90, $91.65, $160.45 and $359.95. What is the total cost of the receivable goods?

Answer:

QUESTION 10

A lawyer's practice charges six different clients the following fees: $889.90, $945.50, $1555.50, $2135.50, $732.50 and $569.25. What is the total of the fees?

Answer:

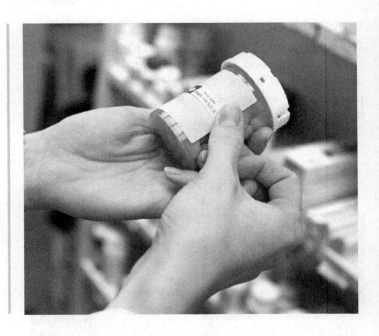

Section B: Subtraction

Short-answer questions

Specific instructions to students

- This section will help you to improve your subtraction skills when working with decimals.
- Read the following questions and answer all of them in the spaces provided.
- You may not use a calculator.
- You need to show all working.

QUESTION 1

A company purchases $18.65 worth of stationery. What change will be given from a $50 note from petty cash?

Answer:

QUESTION 2

An administrative assistant purchases 12 display folders for $21.60. What change will need to go back to petty cash if a $50 note was used to pay for the purchases?

Answer:

QUESTION 3

A part-time receptionist works 18 hours and earns $256.50. The receptionist uses $34.75 for petrol and $84.50 for entertainment. How much is left?

Answer:

QUESTION 4

A building company pays cash for goods. The cost of the goods comes to $198.75. The petty cash box has a total of $313.15. What will the total of the petty cash be after the goods are paid for?

Answer:

QUESTION 5

A receptionist purchases a monthly magazine for their steel company from a newsagent. The cost comes to $114.50. The receptionist pays with three $50 notes. How much change is given?

Answer:

QUESTION 6

The members of a committee want to have a meeting, and drinks and food are to be supplied. The cost of the drinks and food comes to $87.50. There is $133.20 in petty cash. How much will be left once the drinks and food are paid for?

Answer:

QUESTION 7

A receptionist gets paid $568.50 for a week's work. If $178.50 is used to pay for a service on a car, $45.75 is paid for hairdressing and $126 is spent on entertainment, how much money is left?

Answer:

QUESTION 8

A courier delivers two glass tables to a company and requires cash on delivery (COD). The total cost is $456.80. There is $512.40 in petty cash. Once the courier is paid, how much money remains in petty cash?

Answer:

QUESTION 9

Five workers at a screen printing business are paid the following fortnightly wages: $1112.75, $1135.95, $2111.75, $1875.90 and $1450.50. How much will be left in the payroll account, if there was $17 113.90 prior to payment of the wages?

Answer:

QUESTION 10

A CEO of a beverage company is on a salary of $12 240 a month. If the amount in the payroll account for one month is $410 013, how much will be left after the CEO receives the salary?

Answer:

Section C: Multiplication

Short-answer questions

Specific instructions to students

- This section will help you to improve your multiplication skills when working with decimals.
- Read the following questions and answer all of them in the spaces provided.
- You may not use a calculator.
- You need to show all working.

QUESTION 1

If one stamp costs 50 cents, how much will a packet of 50 stamps cost?

Answer:

QUESTION 2

An office uses 38 black pens costing $0.95 each. How much will all 38 pens cost?

Answer:

9780170473866

QUESTION 3

A receptionist purchases three packets of 100 envelopes. If each packet costs $6.50, what is the total?

Answer:

QUESTION 4

An assistant manager purchases eight document folders that cost $6.95 each. How much is the total cost?

Answer:

QUESTION 5

An administrative assistant buys 24 manila folders that cost 90 cents each. What is the total cost?

Answer:

QUESTION 6

Six clients purchase goods from a toy company costing $35.50 each. What is the total?

Answer:

QUESTION 7

Thirteen clients purchase spa covers at a cost of $670.50 each. What would be the total?

Answer:

QUESTION 8

A bridal party has their reception at a hotel. The cost per head is $75.50 and there will be 130 guests. How much will the total bill be?

Answer:

QUESTION 9

A group of 17 Year 12 students are preparing for Schoolies Week. They all decide to stay in the same apartment block and they are offered a package deal by the management. The receptionist makes the booking. The cost per student for the week is $790.90 plus a booking fee of $8.50 per student.

a How much will the total bill be per student, including the booking fee?

Answer:

b How much will the total bill be for the whole group, including the booking fee?

Answer:

QUESTION 10

Twenty-five senior citizens treat themselves to a five-night trip to the Gold Coast. They book a hotel that charges $92.50 per night. The booking fee is $6.50 per person.

a How much does the receptionist charge per person, including the booking fee?

Answer:

b   How much for the whole group, including the booking fee?

Answer:

Section D: Division

Short-answer questions

Specific instructions to students

- This section will help you to improve your division skills when working with decimals.
- Read the following questions and answer all of them in the spaces provided.
- You may not use a calculator.
- You need to show all working.

QUESTION 1

A box contains 24 manila folders which are distributed evenly to eight clients for their documents. How many folders does each client receive?

Answer:

QUESTION 2

A receptionist earns $590.60 for a five-day week. How much is earned per day?

Answer:

QUESTION 3

In a medical clinic, there are 183 folders containing patients' information, which are divided evenly between three filing cabinets. How many will be filed in each cabinet?

Answer:

QUESTION 4

A receptionist working at a wholesale firm needs to allocate money evenly to three events: the Easter show, a mid-year conference and the Christmas show. The management budgets $11 530 for the three events and wants the money distributed evenly. How much does each event get allocated?

Answer:

QUESTION 5

An office assistant working at a roofing factory is asked to purchase eight platters of finger food for a luncheon. The assistant has $140 budgeted for the platters. How much will be allocated for each platter?

Answer:

QUESTION 6

A metal fabrication company is looking to hire two workers. Eight people apply for the two positions and management wants to interview the applicants between 9.00 a.m. and 11.00 a.m. only. How much time does the administrative assistant allocate for each interview if they all have the same amount of interview time?

Answer:

QUESTION 7

A printing company spends $113 on milk, coffee, sugar and tea over one month. What is the overall weekly expenditure for these items?

Answer:

QUESTION 8

A law firm sends eight documents to clients using registered post and the total bill comes to $98. How much, on average, does it cost to send each document?

Answer:

QUESTION 9

Over a month, a travel agency has sales totalling $112 850. What are the average weekly sales?

Answer:

QUESTION 10

A school budgets $211.50 for anti-bullying posters for nine Year 8 classrooms at the beginning of the year. How much money is allocated to each classroom for the posters?

Answer:

Unit 7: Fractions

Section A: Addition

Short-answer questions

Specific instructions to students

- This section is designed to help you to improve your addition skills when working with fractions.
- Read the following questions and answer all of them in the spaces provided.
- You may not use a calculator.
- You need to show all working.

QUESTION 1

$\frac{1}{2} + \frac{4}{5} =$

Answer:

_____

QUESTION 2

$2\frac{2}{4} + 1\frac{2}{3} =$

Answer:

_____

QUESTION 3

An office worker in a medical clinic has three bottles of hand-sanitising lotion that must be divided into four containers. As a fraction, how much will go into each of the four containers?

Answer:

QUESTION 4

A receptionist needs to prepare an invoice for a customer and the number of hours spent on two automotive jobs needs to be calculated. If a mechanic has spent $1\frac{3}{4}$ hours working on one car and $\frac{3}{4}$ of an hour on another car, use fractions to calculate the total time taken on both cars.

Answer:

_____

QUESTION 5

An office assistant spends $1\frac{1}{2}$ hours assisting with a corporate presentation and $1\frac{3}{4}$ hours preparing, sending and recording invoices for work completed by the company. How much time is spent, as a fraction, on these two tasks?

Answer:

_____

Section B: Subtraction

Short-answer questions

Specific instructions to students

- This section is designed to help you to improve your subtraction skills when working with fractions.
- Read the following questions and answer all of them in the spaces provided.
- You may not use a calculator.
- You need to show all working.

QUESTION 1

$\frac{2}{3} - \frac{1}{4} =$

Answer:

QUESTION 2

$2\frac{2}{3} - 1\frac{1}{4} =$

Answer:

QUESTION 3

An accountant spends $1\frac{1}{4}$ hours organising the payroll for a school. Adjustments need to be made for sick leave and carer's leave. Use fractions to show how much time is left for the accountant to work, assuming that they work an eight-hour day.

Answer:

_____

QUESTION 4

An office manager takes $2\frac{1}{2}$ hours to organise a major presentation for a building company. Use fractions to show how many hours are left in the day, if the office manager works an eight-hour day.

Answer:

_____

QUESTION 5

One afternoon, a medical receptionist needed to reorganise and re-file all of the patient's records. If this task took $1\frac{1}{4}$ hours and there were four hours left to work, use fractions to show how much time remains.

Answer:

Section C: Multiplication

Short-answer questions

Specific instructions to students

- This section is designed to help you to improve your multiplication skills when working with fractions.
- Read the following questions and answer all of them in the spaces provided.
- You may not use a calculator.
- You need to show all working.

QUESTION 1

$\frac{2}{4} \times \frac{2}{3} =$

Answer:

_____

QUESTION 2

$2\frac{2}{3} \times 1\frac{1}{2} =$

Answer:

_____

QUESTION 3

An office assistant takes $\frac{3}{4}$ of an hour each day on data entry for noting absentees at a school. If this task is undertaken each school day, use fractions to calculate the total time taken on data entry for a week.

Answer:

_____

9780170473866

QUESTION 4

A travel agent takes $1\frac{1}{2}$ hours each day to research travelling in Europe. If the travel agent works six days each week, use fractions to calculate the total amount of time that is spent on this task.

Answer:

QUESTION 5

An administrative assistant spends $2\frac{1}{2}$ hours each week on organising and calculating the payroll for a major bus manufacturing company. Use fractions to calculate how much time is spent on this task each month.

Answer:

Section D: Division

QUESTION 1

$\frac{2}{3} \div \frac{1}{4} =$

Answer:

QUESTION 2

$2\frac{3}{4} \div 1\frac{1}{3} =$

Answer:

QUESTION 3

A receptionist takes $\frac{1}{4}$ of an hour to update and file one patient's medical records. How many records could be updated and filed in four hours?

Answer:

QUESTION 4

A school assistant has three empty bottles and two full bottles of hand lotion. The hand lotion needs to be transferred from the two full bottles to the three empty bottles evenly. As a fraction, how much hand lotion will be evenly transferred to each of the three empty bottles from the two full bottles?

Answer:

QUESTION 5

A car company is hosting a golf day and the receptionist is asked to assist. If there are two full bottles of sunscreen that need to be poured into six empty bottles, how much will be poured into each of the six empty bottles, as a fraction?

Answer:

Unit 8: Percentages

10% rule: Move the decimal one place to the left to get 10%.

EXAMPLE

10% of $45.00 would be $4.50

QUESTION 1

A receptionist buys stationery at an office supplies store for $22.00. There is a '10% off' sale on.

a   What will the discount be?

Answer:

b   What will the bill come to after the 10% is taken off?

Answer:

QUESTION 2

A hotel advertises that it will deduct 20% off the final cost of three nights' accommodation if people book at a certain time of the year. A receptionist takes a booking that totals $330.00.

a   How much will the discount be?

Answer:

b   What is the final total for the three nights of accommodation?

Answer:

QUESTION 3

A travel agency has a '30% off' sale on flights to Europe. An agent takes a booking for a flight that costs $1200.00.

a   How much will the discount be?

Answer:

b   What will be the final cost?

Answer:

QUESTION 4

A receptionist at a law firm buys three filing cabinets for the practice. The total price comes to $360.80. A 5% discount is given.

a   How much is the discount worth?

Answer:

b   What is the final total? (Hint: Find 10%, halve it then subtract it from the overall price.)

Answer:

QUESTION 5

A legal secretary purchases two sandwich platters for $12, a new desk for $63 and four chairs for $120 at a '20% off' sale.

a   How much is the total of the purchase?

Answer:

b   How much would a 20% discount be?

Answer:

c What is the final cost after the discount?

Answer:

QUESTION 6

The following items are purchased for a hospital by the purchasing officer: 24 white sheets for $162, 15 sets of pillow covers for $187.50, 12 mattress covers for $312, two chairs for $32 and four vases for $56.

a What is the total?

Answer:

b What would a 10% discount be?

Answer:

c What is the final cost after the discount?

Answer:

QUESTION 7

A store offers '20% off' the price of any stationery as long as the customer spends at least $100. If a customer spent $105, how much would six binders originally costing $39 be after the discount?

Answer:

QUESTION 8

A particular range of vertical files is discounted by 15%. The recommended retail price of 100 vertical files is $248.

a How much will the discount be?

Answer:

b What is the final price?

Answer:

QUESTION 9

A secretary needs to buy bottles of sanitised hand lotion for the toilets and bathrooms at work. The bottles are priced at $16.90 each. The store has a '20% off' sale on this item. What will the sale price be?

Answer:

QUESTION 10

Several styles of folders are priced at $5.90 each. During a sale the product is sold at '30% off'. What will the selling price be?

Answer:

Unit 9: Measurement Conversions

QUESTION 1

How many millimetres are there in 1 cm?

Answer:

_____

QUESTION 2

How many centimetres are there in 1 m?

Answer:

_____

QUESTION 3

How many millimetres are there in 1 m?

Answer:

_____

QUESTION 4

If two documents are allowed in each folder, how many documents would there be in 10 folders?

Answer:

_____

QUESTION 5

How many millilitres are there in a 1.5 L bottle of hand lotion?

Answer:

_____

QUESTION 6

A 3500 mL bottle of purified water makes up how many litres?

Answer:

_____

QUESTION 7

An oak boardroom table weighs a quarter of a tonne. How many kilograms is that?

Answer:

_____

QUESTION 8

A delivery truck weighs 2 t. How many kilograms is that?

Answer:

_____

QUESTION 9

A truck weighs 4750 kg. How many tonnes is that?

Answer:

_____

QUESTION 10

A warehouse floor measures 4.8 m wide and 12 m long. How far is it around the perimeter of the warehouse?

Answer:

_____

> From time to time, it will be important to be able to convert inches to centimetres.
>
> Remember: 1 inch = 2.54 cm
> (you can round this down to 2.5 cm if you wish.)

QUESTION 11

Convert 2 inches into centimetres.

Answer:

_____

QUESTION 12

Convert 3 inches into centimetres.

Answer:

QUESTION 13

Convert 4 inches into centimetres.

Answer:

QUESTION 14

Convert 5 inches into centimetres.

Answer:

QUESTION 15

Convert $3\frac{1}{2}$ inches into centimetres.

Answer:

QUESTION 16

Convert 5 cm into inches.

Answer:

QUESTION 17

Convert 10 cm into inches.

Answer:

QUESTION 18

Convert 50 cm into inches.

Answer:

QUESTION 19

Convert 12.5 cm into inches.

Answer:

QUESTION 20

Convert 2.5 cm into inches.

Answer:

Distance		
1 inch	= 2.54 centimeters	= 25.4 millimeters
1 foot	= 0.35 meter	= 30.48 centimeters
1 yard	= 0.9244	
1 mile	= 1.61 kilometers	= 5.280 feet
1 kilometer	= 1,000 meters	= 0.6214 mile
1 meter	= 100 centimeters	= 1,000 mililiters
1 meter	= 3.28 feet	
1 centimeter	= 0.3937 inch	= 10 millimeters
1 millimeter	= 0.039 inch	= 0.1 centimeter
1 micron	= 10^4 centimeter	= 10^5 meter
10^6 meter	= 1 micrometer	
Volume		
1 kiloliter	= 1,000 liters	= 1 cubic meter
1 liter	= 1,000 mililiters	= 1,000 cc
1 milliliter	+ 1 cc (exactly 1.000027 cc)	
1 fluid ounce	= 29.57 mililiters	
1 US gallon	= 3.785 liters	
1 Imperial gallon	= 1 micrometer	
Weight		
1 kilogram	= 1,000 liters	= 2.2 pounds
1 gram	= 1,000 miligrams	= 0.035 ounce
1 milligram	= 1,000 micrograms	= 1/1,000 gram
1 microgram	= 10^6 grams	= 1/1,000 miligram
1 nanogram	= 10^6 grams	= 1/1,000 micogram
1 pound	= 0.45 kilogram	= 16 ounces
1 ounce	= 28.35 grams	

Unit 10: Earning Wages

Short-answer questions

Specific instructions to students

- This unit will help you to calculate how much a job is worth and how long you need to complete the job.
- Read the following questions and answer all of them in the spaces provided.
- You may not use a calculator.
- You need to show all working.

QUESTION 1

A part-time receptionist earns $360.60 net (take home per week). How much does this person earn per year if this is the regular weekly salary? (Remember, there are 52 weeks a year.)

Answer:

QUESTION 2

Suzette is a part-time accountant at a glass manufacturing company. She starts work at 8.00 a.m. and has a break at 10.30 a.m. for 20 minutes. Lunch starts at 12.30 p.m. and finishes at 1.30 p.m. Then Suzette works through to 4.00 p.m.

a   How long are the breaks in total?

Answer:

b   How many hours have been worked in total, excluding breaks?

Answer:

QUESTION 3

Linda works as a school assistant and earns $12.50 an hour. She works a 38-hour week. How much are her gross earnings per week (before tax)?

Answer:

QUESTION 4

Melissa is an administrative assistant and gets paid $411 net for her week's work. From this, she buys petrol which costs $36.95, jewellery worth $19.55, CDs worth $59.97 and a new dress that costs $57.50. She also spends $95 on entertainment.

a   What is the total of all money spent?

Answer:

b   How much is left?

Answer:

QUESTION 5

Interviews for a new position at a law firm are conducted on a Monday morning. The interviews vary in length of time. One goes for 34 minutes, whereas the others go for 18 minutes, 57 minutes, 44 minutes and 59 minutes respectively. How much time, in minutes and hours, has been taken for the interviews?

Answer:

QUESTION 6

A medical receptionist needs to collect, sort and file a number of patients' records. This takes the receptionist $1\frac{1}{4}$ hours to complete.

a   How many minutes is this?

Answer:

_____

b   How many hours are left, if the medical receptionist normally works an eight-hour day?

Answer:

_____

QUESTION 7

An assistant accountant needs to compile the weekly payroll which takes $1\frac{1}{2}$ hours to complete. Following this, work needs to be completed on data entry of stock which takes a further $1\frac{1}{4}$ hours.

a   How many hours were spent on the two tasks? State your answer as a fraction.

Answer:

_____

b   If the assistant accountant works an eight-hour day, how many hours are there left to work in the day, including breaks?

Answer:

_____

QUESTION 8

A receptionist prepares invoices for customers that have had electrical work completed. This takes the receptionist 1 hour 50 minutes to complete.

a   How long, in hours and minutes, will be left in an eight-hour working day?

Answer:

_____

b   How many minutes will the task take?

Answer:

_____

QUESTION 9

An administrative assistant begins work at 7.00 a.m. and works until 4. p.m. He takes a morning break for 20 minutes, a lunch break for 60 minutes and an afternoon break of 20 minutes.

a   How much time has been spent on breaks?

Answer:

_____

b   How much time has been spent working?

Answer:

_____

QUESTION 10

The invoice for work that has been completed by a screen-printing business comes to $1850.50. What would the hourly rate be if the workers had spent 10 hours on the work?

Answer:

_____

Section A: Introducing square numbers

Short-answer questions

Specific instructions to students

- This section is designed to help you to improve your skills and increase your speed in squaring numbers.
- Read the following questions and answer all of them in the spaces provided.
- You may not use a calculator.
- You need to show all working.

> Any number squared is multiplied by itself.

EXAMPLE

4 squared = $4^2 = 4 \times 4 = 16$

QUESTION 1

$6^2 =$

Answer:

_____

QUESTION 2

$8^2 =$

Answer:

_____

QUESTION 3

$12^2 =$

Answer:

_____

QUESTION 4

$3^2 =$

Answer:

_____

QUESTION 5

$7^2 =$

Answer:

_____

QUESTION 6

$11^2 =$

Answer:

_____

QUESTION 7

$10^2 =$

Answer:

_____

QUESTION 8

$9^2 =$

Answer:

_____

QUESTION 9

$2^2 =$

Answer:

_____

QUESTION 1 0

$4^2 =$

Answer:

_____

Section B: Applying square numbers to the trade

Worded practical problems

Specific instructions to students

- This section is designed to help you to improve your skills and increase your speed in calculating volumes of rectangular or square objects. The worded questions make the content relevant to everyday situations.
- Read the following questions and answer all of them in the spaces provided.
- You may not use a calculator.
- You need to show all working.

QUESTION 1

If there are 5 × 5 vertical folders in a box, how many folders are there in total?

Answer:

QUESTION 2

Six packets of documents sent by registered mail are received by a medical centre. If there are six documents in each packet, how many documents will there be in total?

Answer:

QUESTION 3

There are 12 × 12 liquid paper bottles packed into a box. How many bottles are in the box?

Answer:

QUESTION 4

A warehouse floor has an area that is 15 m × 15 m. How much floor area is this in square metres?

Answer:

QUESTION 5

A box contains colour samples for a textile company. The samples are in rows of 8 × 8. How many samples are there?

Answer:

_____

QUESTION 6

A receptionist unpacks two boxes containing display items. The first box contains 4 × 4 company magazines. The second box contains 3 × 3 colour brochures for display. How many items are there in total?

Answer:

_____

QUESTION 7

A box of new business cards is unpacked by a receptionist. If the cards are packed in a 20 × 20 formation, how many are there?

Answer:

_____

QUESTION 8

An office stocks the following: 5 × 5 packets of black pens, 3 × 3 packets of pencils and 10 × 10 boxes of tissues. How many items of stock are there in total?

Answer:

_____

QUESTION 9

The following items are stocked by a soft drink company and they need to be accounted for during a stocktake: 5 × 5 bottles of distilled water, 5 × 5 bottles of filtered water and 5 × 5 bottles of tonic water. How many bottles are there in total?

Answer:

_____

QUESTION 10

The following items are listed during an office stocktake: 3 × 3 vertical files, 2 × 2 glue sticks, 2 × 2 blue pens and 3 × 3 black pens. How many single items are there in total?

Answer:

_____

Unit 12: Invoices/Bills/Specials

Short-answer questions

Specific instructions to students

- This unit will help you to calculate the details of invoices, bills or specials.
- Read the following questions and answer all of them in the spaces provided.
- You may not use a calculator.
- You need to show all working.

QUESTION 1

A customer makes an appointment to see a dentist. The total comes to $350. The dentist has had a promotion in the local paper that reduces the total cost of visits by 20% for one month only.

a By how much does the dental receptionist need to adjust the final bill?

Answer:

b How much will the final cost be?

Answer:

QUESTION 2

A customer books a trip with a travel agent. The client receives a 10% discount due to a promotion that the travel agency is having.

a If the trip costs $1275, how much will the travel agent need to take off due to the 10% discount?

Answer:

b How much will the trip cost after the discount?

Answer:

QUESTION 3

A building company charges $65.50 as a call-out fee. The first hour is charged at $80. Each quarter hour after that is charged at $25. If the builder works for three hours, how much will the receptionist invoice the customer for?

Answer:

QUESTION 4

A client is charged for electrical work completed at their house. The call-out fee is $60. If the electrician takes two hours to install three lights and the hourly rate is $85, how much will the invoice be?

Answer:

QUESTION 5

A landscaping business charges $42 per hour per person for their services. If three landscapers spend $3\frac{1}{2}$ hours working in the backyard of a property, how much will the owner be charged?

Answer:

QUESTION 6

A company receives the following goods: masking tape for $12.60, a new printer for $145.00 and 50 vertical files with tabs for $39.95. A 15% voucher is included as a one-off special for an end-of-financial-year sale.

a How much is the total before the discount?

Answer:

b How much is the discount?

Answer:

c What is the final cost?

Answer:

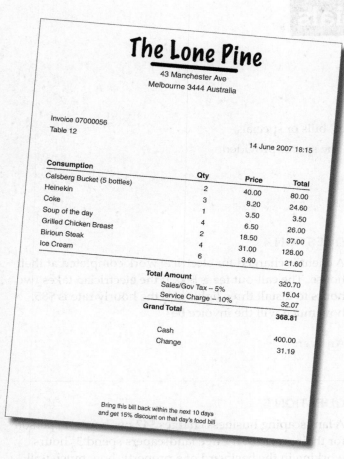

The Lone Pine

43 Manchester Ave
Melbourne 3444 Australia

Invoice 07000056
Table 12

14 June 2007 18:15

Consumption	Qty	Price	Total
Calsberg Bucket (5 bottles)	2	40.00	80.00
Heinekin	3	8.20	24.60
Coke	1	3.50	3.50
Soup of the day	4	6.50	26.00
Grilled Chicken Breast	2	18.50	37.00
Birioun Steak	4	31.00	128.00
Ice Cream	6	3.60	21.60

Total Amount		320.70
Sales/Gov Tax – 5%		16.04
Service Charge – 10%		32.07
Grand Total		**368.81**

Cash	400.00
Change	31.19

Bring this bill back within the next 10 days
and get 15% discount on that day's food bill

QUESTION 7

A hardware company purchases office supplies. The goods total $224. A '25% off' sale is on.

a   How much is saved?

Answer:

b   What is the final cost?

Answer:

QUESTION 8

Office furniture is purchased by an assistant manager for a smallgoods company. The total cost is $1121.50. A '10% off' voucher is used.

a   How much is the voucher worth?

Answer:

b   What is the final cost?

Answer:

QUESTION 9

Three different customers make purchases at an office supplies store. Each customer also has a '15% off' voucher. The first client purchases a hole punch, filing cabinets, pens, folders and envelopes, spending a total of $264. The second client purchases office furniture, masking tape, highlighter pens, whiteboard markers and vertical files for a total of $158. The third customer purchases graph books, lined books, a petty cash box, and manila and display folders, all for $88.

a   How much is the total purchases for all three customers without the voucher?

Answer:

b   How much will the voucher decrease the cost for each customer?

Answer:

c   What is the final cost for each of the three customers?

Answer:

d   What is the total of the three customer's purchases after the discount?

Answer:

QUESTION 10

Six Year 12 students book in for Schoolies Week with the local travel agent. The six students book rooms at a hotel for six nights on the Gold Coast. The cost per person per night is $95. In addition, the six students book a fishing charter for $68 per person and a skydiving experience for $235 per person. What will be the cost for each student?

Answer:

Business Admin
Practice Written Exam
for the Business Admin Trade

Reading time: 10 minutes

Writing time: 1 hour 30 minutes

Section A: Literacy
Section B: General Mathematics
Section C: Trade Mathematics

QUESTION and ANSWER BOOK

Section	Topic	Number of questions	Marks
A	Literacy	7	23
B	General Mathematics	11	25
C	Trade Mathematics	34	52
		Total 52	Total 100

The sections may be completed in the order of your choice.

NO CALCULATORS are to be used during the exam.

Spelling

Read the passage below and then underline the 20 spelling errors.

10 marks

Greg and Suzette both work in the front ofice of a large law firm. Greg is an administative asistant and Suzette is a personal assistant to the Board of Lawyers. They are required to perchase a number of office supplies and office furnture as the law firm is relocating to the central busness district (CBD). Greg and Suzette desided to visit an office supplier in the CBD. The company had an account with the store and this made purchazing easier.

Greg and Suzette had set a list of items that was needed by the firm and they had to try to purchace the best quality items for the lowest avalable price. Suzette spotted the filing cabinets on the far side of the store and they both made their way over to them. The larger filing cabinets were on special for $260 each and the smaler filing cabinets were on sale for $150 each. Suzette could smell a barrgain when she saw one. She said to Greg, 'We'll get two of the large filing cabinets for $520 rather than get four of the smaller filing cabinets for $600.'

Greg dissagreed. He was more practical. 'The smaller ones will fit better in the front office,' explained Greg.

'There will be plennty of room for the large ones and we will save $80. The boss will be hapy with that', said Suzette.

'They won't fit in the office thogh', Greg respanded.

'You leave that to me!' said Suzette and they both contanued shoping.

Once they payed for their purchases on the company account, Greg and Suzette returned to work with all of their purchases.

Correct the spelling errors by writing them out with the correct spelling below.

_____

_____

Alphabetising

Put the following words into alphabetical order.

7 marks

purchase order	medical records
customer service	filing
boardroom	petty cash
payroll	received goods
general ledger	monthly statement
invoice	denominations
data entry	coin

_____   _____

_____   _____

_____   _____

_____   _____

_____   _____

_____   _____

_____   _____

Comprehension

Short-answer questions

Specific instructions to students

- Read the following passage and answer the questions on the following page.

Sally and Rachel started work at 8.45 a.m. on Thursday. There were many tasks to complete as there were interviews for vacant positions, appointments with the business manager and two presentations taking place in the boardroom today. Six of eight applicants had arrived at reception for interviews and Sally had greeted each person and checked them off a list forwarded to her by email from Caryle, the Human Resources Manager. Meanwhile, Rachel had received a memo asking her to prepare the boardroom for the first of two presentations. The first presentation was by the marketing and sales team to the Board of Directors and it was scheduled to begin at 9.15 a.m. Rachel also had to arrange morning tea, including coffee, tea, bottled water and biscuits, as well as notebooks, pens and pencils so that the participants could take notes on the presentation.

Sally rang Caryle, the Human Resource Manager, and told her that two applicants had not arrived for their interview. Caryle said that the interviews would continue on time and as scheduled. Sally asked the first applicant to move into the interview room and wait for Caryle who was on her way down from her office. Sally returned to reception and began typing letters that she had taken in shorthand from the business manager. The first interview finished after 30 minutes and Caryle asked that the second applicant be escorted into the interview room. This interview only lasted 10 minutes and Caryle continued through the scheduled interviews one by one.

Sally left the office with documents to post when Rachel returned from the boardroom, after taking notes on the presentation. Just then, a courier arrived with two small packages for the business manager. Rachel signed the documentation and recorded the identification numbers of each package. She then made her way to the business manager's office and delivered the packages. Once Sally had arrived back from the post office, Rachel went back to the boardroom to clean up and prepare for the second presentation.

QUESTION 1   2 marks

What three activities that were happening in the morning were Sally and Rachel were involved with?

Answer:

_____

_____

QUESTION 2   1 mark

How many applicants had arrived for their interviews?

Answer:

_____

QUESTION 3   1 mark

Who was presenting the first presentation in the boardroom?

Answer:

_____

QUESTION 4   1 mark

What did Rachel need to arrange for the presentation in the boardroom?

Answer:

_____

_____

QUESTION 5   1 mark

What duties did Rachel have to complete when the packages arrived from the courier?

Answer:

_____

_____

Section B: General Mathematics

QUESTION 1   1 + 1 + 1 = 3 marks

What unit of measurement would you use to measure:

a   denominations of money?

Answer:

_____

b   the temperature of air conditioning?

Answer:

_____

c   the amount of purified water?

Answer:

_____

9780170473866

QUESTION 2   1 + 1 + 1 = 3 marks

Write an example of the following and where it may be found in the business admin industry:

a   percentages

Answer:

_____

b   decimals

Answer:

_____

c   fractions

Answer:

_____

QUESTION 3   1 + 1 = 2 marks

Convert the following units:

a   1 kg to grams

Answer:

_____

b   1500 g to kilograms

Answer:

_____

QUESTION 4   1 mark

Write the following in descending order:

0.7   0.71   7.1   70.1   701.00   7.0

Answer:

_____

QUESTION 5   1 + 1 = 2 marks

Write the decimal number that is between the following:

a   0.1 and 0.2

Answer:

_____

b   1.3 and 1.4

Answer:

_____

QUESTION 6   1 + 1 = 2 marks

Round off the following numbers to two decimal places:

a   5.177

Answer:

_____

b   12.655

Answer:

_____

QUESTION 7   1 + 1 = 2 marks

Estimate the following by approximation:

a   101 × 81 =

Answer:

_____

b   399 × 21 =

Answer:

_____

QUESTION 8   1 + 1 = 2 marks

What do the following add up to?

a $25, $13.50 and $165.50

Answer:

_____

b $4, $5.99 and $229.50

Answer:

_____

QUESTION 9   1 + 1 = 2 marks

Subtract the following:

a   196 from 813

Answer:

_____

b   5556 from 9223

Answer:

_____

QUESION 10   1 + 1= 2 marks

Use division to solve:

a   4824 ÷ 3 =

Answer:

_____

b   84.2 ÷ 0.4 =

Answer:

QUESTION 11   2 + 2 = 4 marks

Using BODMAS, solve:

a $(3 \times 7) \times 4 + 9 - 5 =$

Answer:

_____

b $(8 \times 12) \times 2 + 8 - 4 =$

Answer:

Section C: Trade Mathematics

Basic Operations

Addition

QUESTION 1   1 mark

A receptionist purchases 36 vertical files with tabs, 144 whiteboard markers and 25 envelopes. How many items have been purchased in total?

Answer:

QUESTION 2   1 mark

Three documents are forwarded to clients, costing $15, $14 and $17 to post respectively. What are the total postage charges?

Answer:

Subtraction

QUESTION 1   1 mark

A company uses 57 manila folders from a box that contains 150 manila folders. How many remain?

Answer:

QUESTION 2   1 mark

An administrative assistant purchases office supplies that total $124. The store takes off a discount of $35 during a sale. How much is the total?

Answer:

Multiplication

QUESTION 1   1 mark

A receptionist orders six platters of sandwiches for a board meeting. If each platter costs $35, what will be the total cost?

Answer:

QUESTION 2   1 mark

Forty-five bottles of mineral water are purchased for a conference. The unit cost of each bottle is $3. What is the total cost?

Answer:

Division

QUESTION 1   1 mark

A company's monthly income is $55 578. What would the average weekly income be for this company?

Answer:

QUESTION 2   1 mark

At a yearly stocktake, a receptionist counts 72 display folders. If 12 display folders are packed into each box, how many boxes are there?

Answer:

Decimals

Addition

QUESTION 1 1 mark

The following office supplies are purchased: a hole punch for $8.95, two bottles of liquid paper for $13.50 and a printer cartridge for $24.50. How much is spent on the purchases in total?

Answer:

QUESTION 2 1 mark

A store sells the following products during an end-of-financial-year sale: staples for $7.95, paper clips for $11.50 and black pens for $12.85. How much is the total for all three?

Answer:

Subtraction

QUESTION 1 1 mark

A receptionist earns $418.50 per week. If $35.95 is spent on clothes and $25.50 is on food, how much is left?

Answer:

QUESTION 2 1 mark

A purchasing officer purchases two printers for $224.50. If the printers are to be paid for with five $50 notes from petty cash, how much change will be given

Answer:

Multiplication

QUESTION 1 1 + 1 = 2 marks

Three documents are posted from a law firm and it costs $7.95 to post each.

a How much does it cost to post all three documents?

Answer:

b What change is given from $50.00?

Answer:

QUESTION 2 1 + 1 = 2 marks

Four $25 gift vouchers are purchased by a company as Christmas gifts for clients at a cost of $28.50 each.

a What is the total?

Answer:

b What change would be given from $120.00, taken out of petty cash?

Answer:

Division

QUESTION 1 2 marks

The monthly income for a textile company is $208 987. What would be the average weekly income?

Answer:

QUESTION 2 2 marks

A luncheon for a board meeting comes to a total of $196 for seven people. How much is this per person?

Answer:

Fractions

QUESTION 1 1 mark

$\frac{1}{4} + \frac{1}{2} =$

Answer:

QUESTION 2 1 mark

$\frac{4}{5} - \frac{1}{3} =$

Answer:

QUESTION 3 1 mark

$\frac{2}{3} \times \frac{1}{4} =$

Answer:

QUESTION 4

1 mark

$\frac{3}{4} \div \frac{1}{2} =$

Answer:

Percentages

QUESTION 1

2 marks

An office furniture store has a '10% off' sale on all items. If a customer purchases items totalling $149.00, what is the final sale price?

Answer:

QUESTION 2

2 marks

Office supplies are discounted by 20% in a store. If the regular retail price of a printer is $120.00, how much will the customer pay after the discount?

Answer:

Measurement Conversions

QUESTION 1

2 marks

How many grams are there in 1.85 kg?

Answer:

QUESTION 2

2 marks

35 mm converts to how many centimetres?

Answer:

Area

QUESTION 1

2 marks

The floor area of a warehouse that stocks office furniture measures 15 m by 6 m. What is the total floor area?

Answer:

QUESTION 2

2 marks

What is the reception area that measures 5.2 m by 3.5 m?

Answer:

Earning Wages

QUESTION 1

2 marks

A part-time receptionist gets paid $15.50 per hour. If the receptionist works 15 hours a week, how much will their gross pay be?

Answer:

QUESTION 2

2 marks

The following payments are received from customers for work completed by an electrical company: $1190, $3350, $1980, $4870 and $5850. What is the total that will be paid to the company?

Answer:

Squaring Numbers

QUESTION 1

2 marks

What is 7^2?

Answer:

QUESTION 2

2 marks

The floor area of a warehouse measures 13 m × 13 m. What is the total floor area?

Answer:

Purchasing

QUESTION 1

2 marks

A company purchases office furniture from a store and receives 20% off for being a valued client. If $1148.60 worth of office furniture is purchased, what will the final cost be to the company once the discount is taken off?

Answer:

QUESTION 2

2 marks

A company purchases office supplies to the total of $434.60. A 15% discount is given by the store. How much is the company charged after the discount?

Answer:

9780170473866

Deals

Lamps are on sale for $38.95 each or you can buy two for $70. Which is the better deal and how much, if any, will be saved?

Answer:

_____

_____

A store sells packets of A4 envelopes for $12.50 or three packets for $35. Which is the better deal and how much, if any, will be saved?

Answer:

_____

_____

Glossary

Accountant   Qualified professional who is skilled at financial reporting and business analysis.

Accounts payable   Record of funds you owe to suppliers and other business creditors for purchases of stock and overheads and other liabilities, including taxes.

Accounts receivable   Record of funds your customers owe you.

Assets   Economic resources owned by a business or company. Assets can be tangible or intangible and include cash in the bank, accounts receivable, shares, property or buildings, equipment, fixtures, stock or stock in production.

Award   Ruling outlining the rights and obligations of employers and the legally binding minimum wage rates and employment conditions for employees.

Balance   Total of funds remaining in an account after accounting for all transactions (deposits and withdrawals).

Balance sheet   Important business document that shows what a business owns and owes at the date shown. Essentially, a balance sheet is a list of business assets and their cost on one side and a list of liabilities and owners' equity (investment in the business) on the other side.

Best practice   Comprehensive, integrated and cooperative approach to the continuous improvement of all facets of an organisation's operations. It is a method by which leading-edge companies manage their businesses to achieve world-class standards of performance.

Bill of sale   Document which formally transfers ownership of property specified in the document from the borrower to the lender, until such time as the debt has been paid in full.

Budget   Estimate of expenses and revenue.

Capital   Total owned and borrowed funds in a business.

Cash   Includes all money in the bank, in the cash drawer and in petty cash. Banknotes, coins, bills and negotiable securities (like cheques) are cash. But so is the money you can draw on demand – your bank accounts or savings accounts also represent cash.

Cash book   Record of cash payments and receipts, shown under various categories.

Cash flow   Flow of internal funds generated within the business as a result of receipts from debtors, payments to creditors, drawings and cash sales.

Cash receipts   Money received by a business from customers.

Formulae and Data

Circumference of a Circle

$C = \pi \times d$

where: C = circumference, π = 3.14, d = diameter

Diameter of a Circle

$d = \dfrac{C}{\pi}$

Where: C = circumference, π = 3.14, d = diameter

Area

$A = l \times b$

Area = length × breadth and is given in square units

Volume of a Cube

$V = l \times w \times h$

Volume = length × width × height and is given in cubic units

Volume of a Cylinder

$V_c = \pi \times r^2 \times h$

Where: V_c = volume of a cylinder, π = 3.14, r = radius, h = height

Times Tables

1	**2**	**3**	**4**
1 × 1 = 1	1 × 2 = 2	1 × 3 = 3	1 × 4 = 4
2 × 1 = 2	2 × 2 = 4	2 × 3 = 6	2 × 4 = 8
3 × 1 = 3	3 × 2 = 6	3 × 3 = 9	3 × 4 = 12
4 × 1 = 4	4 × 2 = 8	4 × 3 = 12	4 × 4 = 16
5 × 1 = 5	5 × 2 = 10	5 × 3 = 15	5 × 4 = 20
6 × 1 = 6	6 × 2 = 12	6 × 3 = 18	6 × 4 = 24
7 × 1 = 7	7 × 2 = 14	7 × 3 = 21	7 × 4 = 28
8 × 1 = 8	8 × 2 = 16	8 × 3 = 24	8 × 4 = 32
9 × 1 = 9	9 × 2 = 18	9 × 3 = 27	9 × 4 = 36
10 × 1 = 10	10 × 2 = 20	10 × 3 = 30	10 × 4 = 40
11 × 1 = 11	11 × 2 = 22	11 × 3 = 33	11 × 4 = 44
12 × 1 = 12	12 × 2 = 24	12 × 3 = 36	12 × 4 = 48

5	**6**	**7**	**8**
1 × 5 = 5	1 × 6 = 6	1 × 7 = 7	1 × 8 = 8
2 × 5 = 10	2 × 6 = 12	2 × 7 = 14	2 × 8 = 16
3 × 5 = 15	3 × 6 = 18	3 × 7 = 21	3 × 8 = 24
4 × 5 = 20	4 × 6 = 24	4 × 7 = 28	4 × 8 = 32
5 × 5 = 25	5 × 6 = 30	5 × 7 = 35	5 × 8 = 40
6 × 5 = 30	6 × 6 = 36	6 × 7 = 42	6 × 8 = 48
7 × 5 = 35	7 × 6 = 42	7 × 7 = 49	7 × 8 = 56
8 × 5 = 40	8 × 6 = 48	8 × 7 = 56	8 × 8 = 64
9 × 5 = 45	9 × 6 = 54	9 × 7 = 63	9 × 8 = 72
10 × 5 = 50	10 × 6 = 60	10 × 7 = 70	10 × 8 = 80
11 × 5 = 55	11 × 6 = 66	11 × 7 = 77	11 × 8 = 88
12 × 5 = 60	12 × 6 = 72	12 × 7 = 84	12 × 8 = 96

9	**10**	**11**	**12**
1 × 9 = 9	1 × 10 = 10	1 × 11 = 11	1 × 12 = 12
2 × 9 = 18	2 × 10 = 20	2 × 11 = 22	2 × 12 = 24
3 × 9 = 27	3 × 10 = 30	3 × 11 = 33	3 × 12 = 36
4 × 9 = 36	4 × 10 = 40	4 × 11 = 44	4 × 12 = 48
5 × 9 = 45	5 × 10 = 50	5 × 11 = 55	5 × 12 = 60
6 × 9 = 54	6 × 10 = 60	6 × 11 = 66	6 × 12 = 72
7 × 9 = 63	7 × 10 = 70	7 × 11 = 77	7 × 12 = 84
8 × 9 = 72	8 × 10 = 80	8 × 11 = 88	8 × 12 = 96
9 × 9 = 81	9 × 10 = 90	9 × 11 = 99	9 × 12 = 108
10 × 9 = 90	10 × 10 = 100	10 × 11 = 110	10 × 12 = 120
11 × 9 = 99	11 × 10 = 110	11 × 11 = 121	11 × 12 = 132
12 × 9 = 108	12 × 10 = 120	12 × 11 = 132	12 × 12 = 144

Multiplication Grid

	1	2	3	4	5	6	7	8	9	10	11	12
1	1	2	3	4	5	6	7	8	9	10	11	12
2	2	4	6	8	10	12	14	16	18	20	22	24
3	3	6	9	12	15	18	21	24	27	30	33	36
4	4	8	12	16	20	24	28	32	36	40	44	48
5	5	10	15	20	25	30	35	40	45	50	55	60
6	6	12	18	24	30	36	42	48	54	60	66	72
7	7	14	21	28	35	42	49	56	63	70	77	84
8	8	16	24	32	40	48	56	64	72	80	88	96
9	9	18	27	36	45	54	63	72	81	90	99	108
10	10	20	30	40	50	60	70	80	90	100	110	120
11	11	22	33	44	55	66	77	88	99	110	121	132
12	12	24	36	48	60	72	84	96	108	120	132	144

Notes

Notes

Notes

Notes

9780170473866